DENVER INTERNATIONAL AIRPORT

PUBLICATION INFORMATION

Altitude Publishing Ltd.
Denver / The Canadian Rockies / Vancouver
12445 East 39th Avenue, Unit 521
Denver, Colorado 80239
800 957-6888

1500 Railway Avenue
Canmore, Alberta T1W 1P6

Extreme care has been taken to ensure that all information presented in this book is current and accurate, yet neither the author nor the publisher can be held responsible for errors.

Cataloging in Publication

Klinglesmith, Dan R., 1955
Denver International Airport
ISBN 1-55265-025-1 (bound)
ISBN 1-55265-024-3 (pbk.)
1. Denver International Airport.
2. Denver International Airport -- Pictorial works. I. Carter, Chris, 1965- II. Title. HE9797.5.U52D47 1999
387.7'36'0978883
C99-910937-5

Photographs:

Hardcover Edition

Front Cover: DIA east entrance at sunset
Frontispiece: DIA at sunset
Pages 2-3: UAL 747/400 prepares for take-off
Back Cover: FAA Control Tower
Endsheets: Computer-generated diagrams of DIA's flight patterns

Softcover Edition

Front Cover: DIA Jeppesen Terminal tents
Frontispiece: DIA at sunset
Pages 2-3: UAL 747/400 prepares for take-off
Back Cover: FAA Control Tower

Publisher	**Stephen Hutchings**
Associate Publishers	**Dan Klinglesmith**
	Patrick Soran
Design/Layout	**Dan Klinglesmith**
Author	**Dan Klinglesmith**
Editor	**Patrick Soran**
Text Editing	**Chuck Cannon**
Financial Management	**Laurie Smith**

Printed and bound in Canada by Friesens, Altona, Manitoba

Altitude GreenTree Program

Altitude Publishing plants twice as many trees as were used in the manufacturing of this book.

CONTENTS

FOREWORD

On behalf of the City and County of Denver, welcome to DIA, Denver International Airport. Located only 30 minutes from the heart of downtown Denver, DIA has become the most recognizable airport in the world, known to travelers for not only its stunning design but also its efficiency and excellent amenities: shopping, dining, and a host of specialty services.

With Denver fast becoming a center for information technology, cable television, computer technology along with a strong work force, a number of companies have made the Denver metropolitan area their home. And having a state-of-the-art airport is one of the major reasons. The citizens of Denver look at DIA as their connection to the world, their link to business trade and gateway to global destinations.

DIA is more than just the terminal building and concourses. It is also a well-planned layout of runways and efficient air traffic patterns. While other airports have seen dramatic increases in flight delays, DIA maintains one of the best on-time performance records of any major airport in the world. Whether it is the snow for which Colorado is famous or the gorgeous summers which attracts most visitors, DIA is equipped to handle virtually any weather situation. And improvements are continuously made.

From the inside or outside, DIA's translucent roof arcing over Elrey B. Jeppesen Terminal is impressive. It rises from the prairie, a sculpted reflection of the majestic Colorado Front Range. At DIA, however, art seems to be at every turn . . . sometimes in the most unusual places. DIA's award-winning art collection lines corridors and walls, hangs from the ceiling, and springs from the floor. Viewed as an art gallery surrounded by runways or an engineering marvel, DIA is designed to please the senses and function extraordinarily well.

An airport is the doorway to its community. Convenient passenger service moves not only leisure travelers, but also ever-growing business traffic. Both scheduled airlines and cargo carriers move more air freight in and out of DIA every day. DIA is truly a vital component in the economic development of 21st-century Colorado and the American West.

Enjoy your time here, wherever your travels take you!

**Wellington E. Webb
Mayor of Denver**

GATEWAY TO THE AMERICAN WEST

"With a good airport, Denver can expect to be one of the great air centers," proclaimed Charles Lindbergh while visiting the Mile High City shortly after his historic 1927 solo transatlantic crossing. Prophetic words, or perhaps simply the sure knowledge of someone who had soared among the clouds, someone who had clearly seen from that vantage point that during the 20th century the airplane—aviation—would profoundly alter the dimensions of the world.

Just as rivers, harbors and access to established routes fashioned the great trading centers of preceding eras, it is airports that will mold commercial economies of the 21st century. Indeed, during the brief span of less than 100 years the Earth became smaller; heretofore geographically isolated points on the globe have become easily accessible. Even locales far from the nearest port could now rival the great urban trade centers of the maritime age.

Denver is just such a place. Situated at the point where the Great Plains wash against the mighty shoulders of the Rocky Mountains, the largest metropolitan area within a 600-mile / 965-kilometer radius is the gateway to the American West. Wilderness areas set with world-class outdoor pursuits await travelers seeking scenic superlatives to match their recreational dreams. And for businesses that know the importance of information, Denver's high concentration of advanced technology businesses assures a powerful link to the global economy. Already, Denver International Airport has the capacity to accommodate 730,000 aircraft operations and 50 million passengers annually. At final build-out sometime in the next century, DIA will easily meet the traveling needs of 100 million people every year.

Denver International Airport is a 21st-century port . . . the air its ocean.

Pages 8-9: *Denver International Airport encompasses 34,000 acres / 13,600 hectares, or 53 square miles / 137 square kilometers. To put that in perspective, DIA is half the size of Denver, twice the size of Manhattan. Several major airports—Dallas/Ft. Worth, Atlanta and Chicago—would fit onto the site with room to spare.*

Right: *Within sight of the Front Range of the Colorado Rocky Mountains, DIA sits on onetime pioneer farmland. In fact, some 20,000 acres / 8,000 hectares of airport land are still leased to ranchers and farmers.*

Above: *DIA's runways, designed to radiate from the terminal and concourses like a pinwheel, facilitate a "flow-through" traffic pattern allowing aircraft to land, taxi to the gate, and take off in one direction. Each runway is located at least 4,300 feet / 1,311 meters from any parallel runway, permitting as many as three arriving aircraft to line up in parallel patterns even during inclement weather.*

From the tower, air traffic controllers can quickly rearrange traffic configurations from north-south runways to east-west runways to maintain aircraft flow during changing weather conditions.

Right: *In this aerial shot looking south, DIA's 327-foot / 100-meter high Federal Aviation Administration control tower rises above Concourse C. Allowing a three-mile / 4.8-kilometer unobstructed view of DIA's airfield, it is the tallest FAA structure in North America.*

Left: *DIA's terminal, three concourses and five runways can accommodate more than 700,000 aircraft operations and 50 million passengers annually.*

Right Top Left: *Denver International Airport was designed for efficient travel. The airfield's 12,000-foot / 3,600-meter long runways are positioned around the terminal and concourses so that taxiing is minimized. Concourses are located far enough apart so that aircraft need not compete for taxiway or pushback space.*

Right Top Right: *International carriers fly scheduled routes between Denver, Europe and Asia as well as Canada and Mexico.*

Right: *The Front Range of the Rocky Mountains reaches skyward west of Denver. DIA is not only the gateway for millions of outdoor enthusiasts heading to Colorado's high country, but also serves as a major regional hub.*

ARCHITECTURE & ART

Latitude: 39 degrees, 50 minutes, 57.8 seconds. Longitude: 104 degrees, 40 minutes, 23.9 seconds. On a clear day, from Jeppesen Terminal's south end, the blue triangular outline of Pikes Peak rises above the horizon. From this mighty mount's summit Katharine Lee Bates drew inspiration for her poem turned American anthem:

> For purple mountains majesties
> Above the fruited plain!
> America! America!
> God shed His grace on thee
> And crown thy good with brotherhood
> From sea to shining sea!

A century later, the space and scale of DIA's dramatic location were not lost on architect Curt Fentress who crafted the terminal's design. The multi-peaked roof fashioned from Teflon-coated fiberglass echoes the geology, history and mythology of the American West: the jagged profile of snow-mantled mountains; the distinctive cone-shape of Native American teepees; the billowing white of thunderheads rolling across the Great Plains; the canvas-topped processions of covered wagons settling new frontiers. Advocates of Denver International Airport envisioned not merely an air facility but also a testament to the city and the region. DIA's architecture creates its own identity recognizable worldwide as Denver, "Queen City of Plains."

Moreover, the sense of place wasn't confined to DIA's structures; the interior is graced with a multimillion dollar art program, one of the largest public art programs in the world. Collectively, the artworks represent a "journey" theme, sometimes incorporated into the architecture itself, referencing the glorious American West landscape and paying homage to the region's history and diversity of people, but always serving as inspirational and contemplative havens for travelers.

Insets, Page 17: Experimental Aviation *by Denver artist Patty Ortiz is comprised of 140 steel "paper airplanes" suspended above the escalators into Jeppesen Terminal.*

Page 18: *DIA's tent roof echos the shapes of mountain peaks along Colorado's Front Range.*

Left: *Dual Meridian by Denver-based artist David Griggs is located in the 10-story atrium of Concourse A. The installation, with its unique orbit-like perspective, commemorates Denver's location at the 105th meridian.*

Right: *Within Concourse B, Alice Adams' Beaded Circle Crossing springs from the lower level on either side of the concourse with arches supporting a canopy of light.*

Above: Interior Garden *of Concourse C by Michael Singer incorporates 5,000 square feet / 465 square meters of sculptural and architectural elements, as well as 7,000 square feet / 650 square meters of inlaid stone pattern on the floor of the train level.*

Left: *This detail of* America, Why I Love Her *shows a portion of a large map of the United States, whose overall design recalls a 1950s-era postcard heralding quirky attractions. Located at the entryway into east Baggage Claim, the work by artist Gary Sweeney pays tribute to the family vacation.*

Right: *Three diptych murals comprise* The Children of the World Dream of Peace *(detail shown here) by artist/activist Leo Tanguma. Located along the west Baggage Claim entryway, the work depicts children from across the globe in situations of tragedy and devastation as well as in harmony and peace.*

Left: *Artist Terry Allen says, "Throughout history, gargoyles and chimeras have been placed high-up on great cathedrals and other architectural marvels of the world to ward off and protect against the sinister forces of bad luck and evil." Allen's fanciful Notre Denver—two bronze gargoyles about the size of impish five-year-olds seated within suitcases—is perched above the east and west Baggage Claim areas.*

Right: Deep Time/Deep Space *by Leni Schwendinger runs for one mile / 1.6 kilometers along the west tunnel of DIA's people-mover train system. Inspired by Colorado's industrial and social history, the installation infuses the shuttle experience with neon-lighted images from related underground regions such as caves and mine shafts, as well as deep space.*

Right: *Artists Juane Quick-To-See Smith and Ken Iwamasa utilized the entire floor of the Jeppesen Terminal Great Hall for their* work Great Hall Floor.

Large-scale light and dark elements set within the terrazzo flooring suggest—through geometric motifs—the four rivers spilling out from Colorado's Rocky Mountain Continental Divide: the Arkansas, the Platte, the Rio Grande and the Colorado.

Above: Spirit of the People *comprises several pieces telling the story of the West's Native Americans through painted and photographic murals, as well as other media. Located throughout International Arrivals and in Jeppesen Terminal, the works portray historical tribal nations: Apache, Arapaho,* Cheyenne, Comanche, Kiowa, Dené, Pawnee, Shoshone, Lakota and Ute, together with Puebloan peoples such as Zuni and Hopi. This work, On Enemy Grounds, *is by Allen Mose, a Dené born and raised in Arizona's Navajo Country.*

Left: *From 1926 to 1932 the Alexander Airplane Company of Englewood, and later Colorado Springs, built 893 Eaglerock aircraft. At the time, Colorado produced more aircraft than any other place in the world.*

NC205Y pictured left hangs in the west end of Concourse B. Members of the Antique Airplane Association of Colorado and Bayport, New York, restored the craft over the course of 25 years, completing the job in 1989.

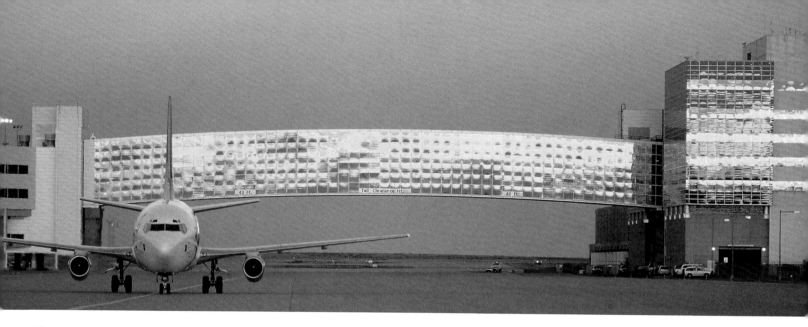

Above: *Spanning 365 feet / 111 meters from Jeppesen Terminal to Concourse A, the Skybridge is the only passenger bridge in the world under which aircraft can pass. Containing two levels, the lower level moves passengers to and from gates while the upper level directs passengers arriving at one of DIA's eight international gates to the* *Federal Inspection Service Area (U.S. Customs, U.S. Immigration and Naturalization, U.S. Department of Agriculture and the U.S. Department of Fish & Wildlife). Both levels of the Skybridge offer spectacular views; to the west the Rocky Mountains and to the east native prairie.*

FLYING THROUGH DIA

Some 1,600 newspaper journalists, TV reporters, radio personalities and other media mavens took to DIA's terminal and concourses for opening day, February 28, 1995. The inauguration of the $4.9 billion facility garnered public praise for its stunning juxtaposition of High Plains perspective and 21st-century edifice.

Center stage goes to Jeppesen Terminal, the equivalent of 36 football fields on seven levels, in all 3.5 million square feet / 325,150 million square meters beneath a canopy of translucent mountain tops. Here is DIA's "town square" complete with check-in counters and baggage claim; shady arbors and fountains; shops and boutiques offering everything from magazines to massage, holograms to handbags; and dozens of concessions, cafes and restaurants to fit any taste. Services range from banking to postal and packing centers. On Level 6 is the DIA Interfaith Chapel, a quiet sanctuary for visitors and employees alike.

The 365-foot / 111-meter long Skybridge arcs across the taxiway from Jeppesen Terminal to Concourse A, but most travelers prefer the "train," DIA's Automated Guideway Transit System (AGTS). The people-mover system operates much like a train (though on rubber tires not steel wheels) with reliable passage to DIA's concourses. As much happy diversion as mere transportation, the AGTS tunnels house evocative art installations. DIA's Concourses A, B and C were designed to accommodate easy and efficient passenger movement amid the comfort and convenience of ample lounge areas near shopping and food courts. "Walkalators" run along the centerline of Concourses A and B, speeding passengers to their gates. DIA's concourses offer more than 100 airline gates for domestic and international arrivals/departures.

It's said that passengers not only fly from DIA, they "fly" through DIA as well. It's worth lingering a while, too.

Pages 30-31: *Artists William Maxwell and Antoinette Rosato incorporated 5,280 propellers into the* Kinetic Light Air Curtain *sculpture viewed while passing through the east train tunnel. Denver, also know as the Mile High City, is exactly 5,280 feet / 1,587 meters above sea level.*

Page 33: *Concourse A subcore floor mosaics by Darrell Anderson and Barb McKee prove to be an ideal spot for both tearful good-byes and hopeful hellos.*

Left: *Nearly 250 volunteer Hospitality Ambassadors sporting white cowboy hats assist travelers at DIA. The friendly and knowledgeable folks have become very popular with airport patrons and the progam is now a model worldwide.*

Above: *Arriving and departing passengers rely on the Automated Guideway Transit System (AGTS). The automated rail system is comprised of two parallel tunnels running north and south through the center of the airport. Stations are located at Jeppesen Terminal and the central cores of Concourses A, B and C.*

Each car is capable of holding 100 passengers and during peak periods more than 6,000 people can be transported per hour in each direction. The roundtrip from Jeppesen Terminal to Concourse C, the maximum distance, takes less than 10 minutes.

The distinctive musical greetings heard by boarding AGTS passengers are Door Chimes *by artist Jim Green. Crafted from traditional western songs such as* Home on the Range, *the melodic interludes precede the AGTS voice announcements.*

Left: *Situated midway between Tokyo, Japan, and Frankfurt, Germany, the Mile High City is strategically located to link air passenger services and cargo markets from Asia to Europe. Further, Denver's mid-continent location offers near-perfect coordinates for airline hub operations serving North and Central American destinations.*

Right: Air Force One *has been a frequent visitor under several presidential administrations. In 1997, Denver hosted the "Summit of the Eight," drawing together presidents and prime ministers from the world's leading industrialized nations.*

Above: *Natural light bathes the Elrey B. "Jepp" Jeppesen Terminal, its fabric roof constructed from translucent Teflon-coated fiberglass. The terminal's 1.5 million square feet / 139,345 square meters are focused around the atrium's expansive Great Hall complete with groves of* *leafy trees gracing the terminal's tranquil north and south lounge areas. Only 10 percent of available light passes through the roof fabric; fiberglass has little mass and does not conduct or store heat.*

Right: *Advanced airport security was an integral component of DIA's overall design and the airport, FAA and airlines continually update methods to ensure the highest public safety. Thousands of people pass through DIA's security inspection areas daily.*

Right: *With more than 35 restaurants, eateries, and beverage proprietors located throughout DIA's Jeppesen Terminal, as well as each concourse, passengers enjoy a wide variety of menu options ranging from quick snacks to leisurely dining.*

Left: *More than 200,000 square feet / 18,580 square meters of Jeppesen Terminal are dedicated to shops and restaurants. High-quality passenger services make spending time here a pleasure. Concessions are highly valued DIA partners and contribute more than $100 million in annual revenue, in addition to creating thousands of jobs for local residents.*

Left: *Although all concourses are similar, Concourse B is longer and wider than Concourses A or C. Concourse B, from end to end, runs 3,300 feet / 990 meters, the equivalent of 11 football fields. "Walkalators" help passengers speed to and from gates and the concourses.*

Above: *The passenger Skybridge from Jeppesen Terminal to Concourse A is 365 feet / 111 meters long, 40 feet / 12 meters wide, and 45 feet / 14 meters high at its midpoint above the taxiway.*

ALL SYSTEMS GO!

From Denver International Airport's initial inception in the late 1980s, planners faced a visionary opportunity: the prospect of not only constructing the first major airport in the United States since the then 20-year-old Dallas-Ft. Worth Airport, but also to build a state-of-the-art air transportation harbor to serve travelers' needs well into the next century.

The concept-to-completion process was described as nothing short of a "cosmic convergence" of many, sometimes conflicting, interests: political, environmental, economic, engineering. In the end, the transformation of pioneer ranch and farmland into the world's most sophisticated airport signified a stunning achievement for the city, Colorado and the nation. The construction of DIA would be one of the world's largest projects undertaken in the last half of the century, rivaling other great transport projects such as the Panama Canal.

The massive endeavor would all be for naught, however, if not for the day-to-day efforts of DIA's 25,000 employees, the majority of whom are seldom seen by the traveling public. The focus, cooperation and commitment required to successfully and safely handle more than 1,300 flights daily to more than 110 nonstop destinations is truly an awesome achievement. It is the work of not only DIA's commercial airlines and air cargo carriers but also FAA air traffic controllers, baggage handlers, snow removal teams, fire personnel, police units, airport administration and management, deicing crews, security guards, customs agents, janitorial staff, Skycaps, postal employees, volunteer Hospitality Ambassadors, physicians and nurses, cashiers, restaurant chefs and waitpeople, . . .

Thanks for making "All Systems Go!" each and every day.

Pages 44-45: *Controllers atop the Federal Aviation Administration control tower watch over DIA traffic using state-of-the-art communications and Doppler radar, allowing technicians to view storm cells from a three-dimensional perspective.*

Right: *DIA's FAA control tower was engineered to sway only a half-inch / 1.26 centimeters in an 86-mile / 138-kilometer-per-hour wind, an unlikely but not impossible situation at the airport's location on the High Plains.*

Within the 87-foot / 26.5-meter diameter, mushroom-top shaped structure, FAA air traffic controllers have an unobstructed view of all DIA runways and taxiways via 1.5 inch / 3.8 centimeter-thick distortion-free windows.

Left: *During normal morning and evening peak traffic periods, DIA easily accommodates more than 90,000 passengers and some 200,000 "meeters and greeters," relatives and friends seeing off and welcoming loved ones and business associates.*

Right: *Control Tower B provides a bird's-eye view for both DIA and airline operations personnel. DIA staff help coordinate gate assignments from this tower and their colleagues at United Airlines do the same for UAL's operations on Concourses B and A.*

Left: *DIA's Automated Baggage System includes 90,000 feet / 27,440 meters of track with 4,000 Destination Coded Vehicles (DCVs) to transport customer luggage to aircraft. The system can move 34,000 pieces of luggage per hour with DCVs zipping along at a maximum speed of 19 miles / 31 kilometers per hour.*

Right Top: *The Denver Police Department provides security for the terminal and concourses in addition to all public areas, roadways and the airfield.*

Right Bottom: *Specially trained firefighters from the Denver Fire Department operate four Aircraft Rescue and Fire Fighting (ARFF) stations; all are staffed 24 hours a day, seven days a week.*

Left: *Rapid response snow removal teams keep DIA operating at peak performance during winter. Teams swiftly clear more than 400 lane miles / 644 lane kilometers of roadway and some five million square yards / 4.1 million square meters of runways, taxiways, aprons and ramp areas.*

Right & Below: *During cold winter weather, three centralized deicing pads accommodate up to six aircraft. Aircraft rarely queue after deicing as the pads are located close to runways and planes may proceed to take-off shortly after leaving the pad. Glycol used during deicing operations is collected and recycled.*

Left: *DIA's Category III Instrument Landing System (ILS) and Surface Movement Guidance Control System (SMGCS) combine to maintain the capacity for multiple flight operations. Ground radar pinpoints the exact locations of taxiing aircraft for controllers, while runway and taxiway lighting systems (some 18,000 lights embedded into runways) guide aircraft during low visibility.*

Right: *While most people experience DIA as airline passengers, the complex also functions as an international commercial hub with air cargo carriers, air freight forwarders, just-in-time delivery companies, as well as U.S. Customs brokers.*

Left: *DIA planners worked with the Environmental Protection Agency and 37 other federal, state and local agencies to construct an airport which conserves resources and minimizes pollution.*

Standard incandescent lighting was largely avoided throughout the vast concourse and terminal areas in favor of 26-watt compact fluorescents which use a fraction of the electricity. Additional energy savings are realized from a computerized "light shedding" system that turns off successive rows of lamps as the sun takes over a share of the lighting load during daylight hours.

To promote clean air, many airport fleet vehicles run on natural gas and DIA's central plant furnaces are equipped with low nitrogen oxide burners and flue gas recirculators, effectively removing an estimated 90 tons / 82,000 kilograms of nitrogen oxide from the air annually.

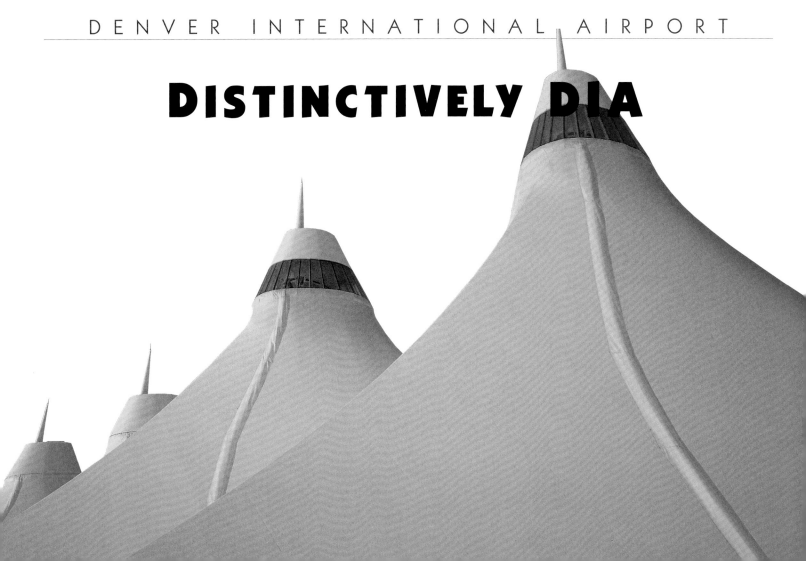

DISTINCTIVELY DIA

Left: *DIA's roof system utilizes a steel cable system similar to that of the Brooklyn Bridge, relying on design curvature and equalization of the fabric's stress fields for stability. The roof membrane weighs 400 tons / 363,000 kilograms.*

Above: *Set atop onetime pioneer farmland, DIA still leases portions of the expansive site to farmers who raise crops such as millet and winter wheat. Further, some 40 oil and natural gas "pumpjacks" dot DIA's landscape. Revenue from these ventures reaches nearly $2 million annually.*

Left: Fenceline Artifact and Pivot Emblem, *located south of Jeppesen Terminal, intersects the landscape with memories of the recent past. In addition to farming implements, artists Lewis "Buster" Simpson and Sherry Wiggins incorporated these birdhouses which are architectural replicas of farmhouses that once occupied the DIA site.*

Right Insets: 21st Century Artifacts, *cast bronze floor insets scattered throughout Concourse B, were inspired by Colorado's rich geological past. Artist team Carolyn Braaksma and Mark Villareal worked with their designs on paper for three years before seeing them set by a terrazzo crew within the span of six weeks.*

Dinosaur fossils were discovered on the DIA excavation site and are now housed in display cases at the north end of Jeppesen Terminal. The Stegosaurus *(shown right) is Colorado's state dinosaur.*

Pages 62-63: *DIA's long profile at sunrise; greeting a new day—and a bright future— along the Colorado Front Range.*

• DIA encompasses 53 square miles / 137 square kilometers.

• The elevation at DIA is 5,425 feet / 1,653 meters above sea level. Downtown Denver is located 23 miles / 37 kilometers southwest of DIA.

• At its construction peak in July 1993, DIA employed more than 11,000 workers.

• A United Airlines Boeing 757 was the first commercial aircraft to land at DIA, guided to its precise automatic touchdown by computer.

• DIA's five runways are each 12,000 feet / 3,600 meters long, 150 feet / 46 meters wide; at least 4,300 feet / 1,311 meters separate the runways from each other.

• The Great Hall of Jeppesen Terminal measures 900 by 210 feet, 274 by 64 meters.

• Construction on Denver International Airport began on September 28, 1989, and the facility officially opened on February 28, 1995. The final price for DIA's construction is officially marked at $4.9 billion.

• More than 100 million tons / 91 billion kilograms of earth were moved during airport construction, nearly a third of the amount moved during the construction of the Panama Canal. If loaded into dumptrucks end to end they'd extend 1.5 times around the globe.

• Runway substructure is 17 inches / 43 centimeters concrete on 8 inches / 20 centimeters of cement-treated base on 12 inches / 30 centimeters of subgrade on 6 feet / 1.8 meters of compacted soil.

• DIA's fiber optic communications spine stretches 5,300 miles / 8,530 kilometers, the distance from New York City to Buenos Aires.

• DIA's environmentally friendly features include recycled deicing fluid, natural gas-powered vehicles, low-flow toilets and xeriscaping.

• Quarries in Marble, Colorado, supplied the white marble used on areas of the terminal walls. Stone from the same quarry was used for the Tomb of the Unknown Soldier and the Lincoln Memorial.

• The fueling system at DIA is capable of pumping 1,000 gallons / 3,785 liters of jet fuel per minute through a 28-mile / 45-kilometers network of pipes. Each of six fuel farm tanks holds 65,000 barrels (2.73 million gallons / 10.3 million liters) of jet fuel.

• United Airlines 1062 bound for Kansas City, MO, was the first commercial departure from DIA; United Airlines 1474 from Colorado Springs, CO, was the first arrival.

• Jeppesen Terminal is named for "Captain Jepp," Elrey Jeppesen, an early aviator known worldwide today for his navigation charts.

• DIA is the world's 10th busiest airport and the 6th busiest in the United States.

• Cable TV titan Bill Daniels experienced DIA's first general aviation landing, touching down in his jet shortly after 12 a.m. on February 28, 1995.

Chris Carter

An employee of the City and County of Denver's Department of Aviation since 1992, Chris Carter began taking still photographs and shooting videotape of Denver International Airport during its construction. His photographs of DIA have appeared in newspapers, magazines and brochures throughout the world. A self-taught photographer, Carter began his career in 1987 as a broadcast journalist for the U.S. Navy.

Acknowledgement

"A special thanks goes to airport maintenance and operations. Without their kind efforts the images presented in this book could not have been made. I would especially like to thank Dan Melfi, Assistant Deputy Manager of Aviation, Marketing. His vision made this pictorial celebration of DIA a reality."

Chris Carter

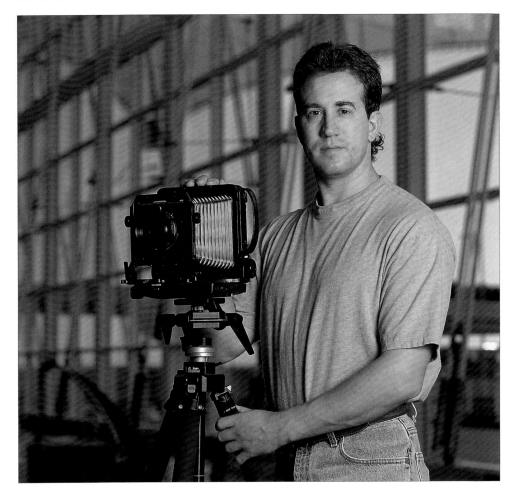